Practice Arithmetic with Decimals Workbook

Improve Your Math Fluency Series

Chris McMullen, Ph.D.

Practice Arithmetic with Decimals Workbook
Improve Your Math Fluency Series

Copyright (c) 2010 Chris McMullen, Ph.D.

All rights reserved. This includes the right to reproduce any portion of this book in any form. However, teachers who purchase one copy of this book, or borrow one physical copy from a library, may make and distribute photocopies of selected pages for instructional purposes for their own classes only. Also, parents who purchase one copy of this book, or borrow one physical copy from a library, may make and distribute photocopies of selected pages for use by their own children only.

CreateSpace

Nonfiction / Education / Elementary School / Arithmetic
Children's / Science / Mathematics / Arithmetic
Professional & Technical / Education / Specific Skills / Mathematics

ISBN: 145362693X

EAN-13: 9781453626931

Practice Arithmetic with Decimals Workbook

Contents

Multiplication Table	4
Making the Most of this Workbook	5
Part 1: Practice Adding Numbers with Decimals	6
Part 2: Practice Subtracting Numbers with Decimals	27
Part 3: Practice Multiplying Numbers with Decimals	48
Part 4: Practice Long Division with Decimals – Level I	69
Part 5: Practice Long Division with Decimals – Level II	90
Answer Key	111

Multiplication Table

	1	2	3	4	5	6	7	8	9	10
1	1	2	3	4	5	6	7	8	9	10
2	2	4	6	8	10	12	14	16	18	20
3	3	6	9	12	15	18	21	24	27	30
4	4	8	12	16	20	24	28	32	36	40
5	5	10	15	20	25	30	35	40	45	50
6	6	12	18	24	30	36	42	48	54	60
7	7	14	21	28	35	42	49	56	63	70
8	8	16	24	32	40	48	56	64	72	80
9	9	18	27	36	45	54	63	72	81	90
10	10	20	30	40	50	60	70	80	90	100

Making the Most of this Workbook

- Mathematics is a language. You can't hold a decent conversation in any language if you have a limited vocabulary or if you are not fluent. In order to become successful in mathematics, you need to practice until you have mastered the fundamentals and developed fluency in the subject. This *Practice Arithmetic with Decimals Workbook* will help you improve the fluency with which you add, subtract, multiply, and divide numbers with decimals, including long division.

- You may need to consult the multiplication table on page 4 occasionally as you begin your practice, but should refrain from relying on it. Force yourself to solve the problems independently as much as possible. It is necessary to memorize the basic multiplication facts and know them quickly in order to become successful at multiplying and dividing numbers with decimals.

- This book is conveniently divided into 5 parts: Part 1 is focused on adding numbers with decimals, Part 2 is focused on subtracting numbers with decimals, Part 3 is focused on multiplying numbers with decimals, and Parts 4 and 5 are focused on long division with decimals (long division is separated into two sections, Part 4 being somewhat simpler and Part 5 being somewhat more involved). This way you can master one basic skill at a time.

- Each chapter begins with a concise set of instructions describing how to add, subtract, multiply, or divide numbers with decimals. These instructions are followed by a couple of examples. Use these examples as a guide until you become fluent in the technique.

- After you complete a page, check your answers with the answer key in the back of the book. Practice makes permanent, but not necessarily perfect: If you practice making mistakes, you will learn your mistakes. Check your answers and learn from your mistakes such that you practice solving the problems correctly. This way your practice will make perfect.

- Math can be fun. Make a game of your practice by recording your times and trying to improve on your times, and recording your scores and trying to improve on your scores. Doing this will help you see how much you are improving, and this sign of improvement can give you the confidence to succeed in math, which can help you learn to enjoy this subject more.

Part 1: Practice Adding Numbers with Decimals

To add numbers with decimals, stack them vertically and align their decimal points. Then add the numbers the same way that you would add whole numbers. It is important to align the sum (that's the answer) with the addends (the two numbers that you are adding together) such that the positions of the decimal points match. This way, the decimal positions of the sum (that's the answer) will match the decimal positions of the addends. Remember to include the decimal point in your answer. Study the examples below and refer to them as needed to guide your practice – until you can solve the problems by yourself. When you complete a page of exercises, check your answers in the back of the book – and learn from any mistakes that you might have made.

EXAMPLES

$$4.23 + 0.078 = \qquad 0.449 + 0.035 =$$

$$\begin{array}{r} \overset{1}{4.23} \\ +\,0.078 \\ \hline 4.308 \end{array} \qquad \begin{array}{r} \overset{1}{0.449} \\ +\,0.035 \\ \hline 0.484 \end{array}$$

Notice that these decimals end with undeclared repeating zeroes. That is, the number 4.23 can also be written as 4.230 or 4.2300 and so on. You may add trailing zeroes to a number with decimals if you find it to be helpful. (Don't add zeroes anywhere else, though. For example, 0.04 and 0.4 are not the same.)

Practice Arithmetic with Decimals Workbook

38.9 + 4 =   1.019 + 80 =   0.8 + 31.9 =

0.475 + 76.2 =   3.394 + 46.02 =   7.896 + 0.004 =

0.057 + 64.27 =   989 + 7.8 =   471.8 + 538 =

8.3 + 36.76 =   0.3 + 987 =   2.512 + 48 =

0.07 + 0.026 =   379 + 28.2 =   35 + 93 =

0.9 + 7 =   92.16 + 0.079 =   3.149 + 55 =

Improve Your Math Fluency Series

0.02 + 0.17 =   0.865 + 0.337 =   0.01 + 3.18 =

0.01 + 2.958 =   24.9 + 8.77 =   75.5 + 778.6 =

0.218 + 0.093 =   0.058 + 2396 =   6.5 + 85.59 =

0.02 + 3 =   451.7 + 0.2 =   0.066 + 46.1 =

892.6 + 8.2 =   6.922 + 7.361 =   0.097 + 1.93 =

2589 + 8.5 =   76.6 + 1.8 =   0.11 + 8.821 =

Practice Arithmetic with Decimals Workbook

0.853 + 30 =   89.7 + 7.361 =   165 + 0.28 =

7.238 + 9.27 =   6.79 + 863 =   0.9 + 0.009 =

0.7 + 0.727 =   4.6 + 15 =   4.4 + 0.09 =

33.8 + 426 =   3.6 + 89.8 =   372.7 + 5842 =

59.8 + 0.36 =   23.2 + 0.02 =   24.69 + 0.079 =

0.021 + 9.155 =   0.09 + 4.511 =   2.041 + 5.8 =

Improve Your Math Fluency Series

0.063 + 3.012 =   0.089 + 0.589 =   5.971 + 0.03 =

0.802 + 1.5 =   0.89 + 7618 =   6001 + 7.077 =

0.028 + 0.077 =   0.89 + 75.6 =   0.35 + 3.1 =

0.01 + 69 =   2 + 0.008 =   0.22 + 32.6 =

2527 + 0.505 =   6.8 + 95 =   6.009 + 6.11 =

784.9 + 0.184 =   0.11 + 1.61 =   9 + 1612 =

Practice Arithmetic with Decimals Workbook

0.006 + 2.2 =	0.038 + 520.4 =	0.055 + 0.06 =
0.056 + 9 =	97.1 + 773.8 =	0.64 + 2.226 =
4.109 + 0.02 =	0.07 + 7.1 =	57 + 0.06 =
619 + 0.004 =	3.7 + 30.8 =	0.091 + 542 =
0.02 + 6.37 =	0.004 + 7 =	1 + 0.01 =
498 + 3.81 =	4349 + 0.75 =	577 + 72.38 =

Improve Your Math Fluency Series

37 + 0.083 = 3.351 + 7 = 14.99 + 0.36 =

0.09 + 6.806 = 4.088 + 0.02 = 3.98 + 0.002 =

79.2 + 9.35 = 0.002 + 7.62 = 7.922 + 0.003 =

9.153 + 0.4 = 65.9 + 0.2 = 0.1 + 0.07 =

1 + 27 = 2248 + 58 = 25.02 + 6.6 =

0.04 + 22 = 0.3 + 84 = 4.74 + 1.436 =

Practice Arithmetic with Decimals Workbook

33 + 0.8 =   0.009 + 0.048 =   0.879 + 752.1 =

1.6 + 161 =   2.54 + 7.157 =   504 + 18.3 =

5.463 + 56 =   410.8 + 0.004 =   24.9 + 0.9 =

526 + 59.69 =   345.9 + 0.015 =   52.6 + 36.8 =

496.5 + 0.135 =   6.6 + 699 =   3.48 + 419 =

804 + 4.255 =   0.02 + 8.77 =   14.28 + 5580 =

Improve Your Math Fluency Series

0.003 + 774.7 =   9.62 + 304.5 =   4.657 + 30 =

5.1 + 0.07 =   3820 + 0.001 =   6.8 + 9733 =

0.003 + 0.34 =   0.9 + 0.8 =   5.02 + 99 =

55.8 + 99 =   0.34 + 2.293 =   6.6 + 59.31 =

0.09 + 90.58 =   0.11 + 31 =   3 + 0.9 =

99 + 0.06 =   5.869 + 862 =   0.2 + 0.27 =

Practice Arithmetic with Decimals Workbook

0.56 + 221.8 =   9010 + 0.4 =   3220 + 1.2 =

0.96 + 0.026 =   0.001 + 216 =   8.3 + 7 =

0.009 + 3.43 =   32.38 + 0.05 =   4.15 + 7 =

738 + 0.2 =   0.2 + 0.095 =   7.24 + 8353 =

0.12 + 1.64 =   58.1 + 16 =   776.5 + 0.68 =

5 + 0.006 =   0.07 + 6441 =   2 + 80.59 =

Improve Your Math Fluency Series

75.6 + 5893 =   0.05 + 0.003 =   0.63 + 72.93 =

42.23 + 0.05 =   887.1 + 0.003 =   2.683 + 3.65 =

515.2 + 62 =   3 + 5.54 =   0.02 + 14 =

9 + 8.815 =   313 + 0.044 =   0.033 + 0.04 =

0.038 + 863 =   0.24 + 44.4 =   4.5 + 5809 =

0.94 + 7245 =   2.2 + 0.203 =   5 + 92 =

Practice Arithmetic with Decimals Workbook

39.3 + 3.9 =   0.168 + 0.46 =   0.8 + 709 =

0.33 + 744.3 =   0.45 + 0.6 =   7073 + 0.9 =

0.185 + 9.019 =   0.808 + 0.072 =   78.07 + 813.5 =

0.54 + 535 =   0.4 + 4.29 =   6.673 + 0.522 =

69 + 889.5 =   6.895 + 9390 =   43.3 + 0.6 =

0.879 + 0.076 =   2.3 + 237 =   0.4 + 36.53 =

12.07 + 5 =	640.6 + 2.2 =	8.802 + 3 =
0.06 + 4.8 =	6081 + 0.018 =	94 + 0.09 =
7.71 + 0.5 =	58.75 + 4 =	2.1 + 0.6 =
372 + 7.5 =	0.932 + 0.003 =	0.45 + 0.54 =
0.6 + 93 =	9.605 + 0.037 =	1.48 + 0.324 =
3 + 0.039 =	396.7 + 0.22 =	78.18 + 19.75 =

Practice Arithmetic with Decimals Workbook

987 + 0.007 =		0.828 + 62 =		83.03 + 0.6 =

15 + 82 =		0.407 + 80.92 =		73 + 0.4 =

3.11 + 0.802 =		645.7 + 484 =		0.006 + 63.3 =

0.054 + 2.91 =		0.06 + 0.18 =		0.2 + 86.4 =

0.4 + 217.4 =		0.93 + 0.07 =		38.2 + 2.01 =

8.9 + 6.9 =		30.09 + 0.08 =		0.006 + 4.54 =

Improve Your Math Fluency Series

3.46 + 7.5 =   9.48 + 7.97 =   0.06 + 0.08 =

75 + 87.6 =   5.777 + 0.7 =   0.01 + 90.54 =

15.28 + 3363 =   22 + 0.85 =   3569 + 0.04 =

0.01 + 0.09 =   0.655 + 0.058 =   4.84 + 63.4 =

5724 + 31.82 =   0.02 + 5.08 =   0.09 + 18.6 =

43.73 + 9 =   261 + 0.009 =   407.9 + 3.8 =

Practice Arithmetic with Decimals Workbook

5.09 + 0.036 =		3 + 0.08 =		9 + 0.23 =

0.5 + 4255 =		0.04 + 0.06 =		7.789 + 0.96 =

633.5 + 0.099 =		413.5 + 8.726 =		4.69 + 38.1 =

0.038 + 7.221 =		97.21 + 40 =		9.47 + 8.9 =

0.277 + 0.626 =		29.4 + 2083 =		5 + 0.005 =

2 + 0.02 =		38 + 0.3 =		9486 + 7.3 =

7 + 2.639 =   81.3 + 5.6 =   8.3 + 0.2 =

232 + 0.2 =   0.01 + 5.3 =   0.04 + 14.25 =

3.052 + 274 =   186.1 + 0.72 =   0.041 + 55 =

0.05 + 58 =   1.54 + 0.037 =   48.99 + 0.335 =

0.398 + 0.7 =   4.4 + 7836 =   3.317 + 6.337 =

61 + 6.006 =   6.3 + 0.3 =   5 + 8.739 =

Practice Arithmetic with Decimals Workbook

4325 + 20.6 =   0.003 + 23.9 =   0.07 + 7.589 =

4.15 + 704.2 =   0.63 + 0.63 =   9.62 + 2559 =

0.009 + 108 =   9.84 + 0.04 =   0.03 + 8 =

9.88 + 0.097 =   0.905 + 9.54 =   6.63 + 3 =

0.043 + 2.41 =   0.52 + 0.02 =   872 + 539.8 =

0.03 + 0.68 =   0.019 + 41.67 =   6.56 + 49.71 =

Improve Your Math Fluency Series

2 + 61.42 =		0.58 + 3.055 =		22 + 0.3 =

98.6 + 0.7 =		1.318 + 0.2 =		6490 + 0.81 =

39 + 2.1 =		6 + 6.55 =		868 + 0.5 =

37 + 0.058 =		0.8 + 6.43 =		0.02 + 365 =

9263 + 0.019 =		0.01 + 0.002 =		60.6 + 2.875 =

1.66 + 6.858 =		2 + 90.9 =		0.03 + 533.3 =

Practice Arithmetic with Decimals Workbook

724.2 + 123 =		0.004 + 47 =		69.3 + 1.04 =

7788 + 53.89 =		84 + 5.2 =		19 + 0.06 =

0.13 + 0.301 =		6737 + 8.695 =		0.002 + 0.15 =

0.79 + 0.66 =		4.79 + 9 =		17.67 + 81.8 =

14 + 0.09 =		43.5 + 73 =		7 + 409.2 =

0.023 + 616 =		22.6 + 0.036 =		5.6 + 0.082 =

Improve Your Math Fluency Series

34.38 + 75.6 =   7.465 + 0.49 =   0.36 + 7.246 =

72.9 + 9.6 =   0.86 + 6.3 =   0.5 + 2.3 =

65.16 + 0.947 =   1.72 + 0.772 =   6.362 + 9.859 =

2 + 98 =   5.8 + 0.63 =   76.9 + 2 =

0.021 + 83.16 =   113.9 + 2 =   6.59 + 54.7 =

6579 + 5.2 =   1.59 + 6.1 =   7.1 + 5112 =

Part 2: Practice Subtracting Numbers with Decimals

Like adding numbers with decimals, subtract numbers with decimals by stacking them vertically and aligning their decimal points. Add trailing zeroes to the minuend (that's the top number) or subtrahend (that's the number you are subtracting) if necessary so that the minuend and subtrahend match in final decimal position. Then subtract the numbers the same way that you would subtract whole numbers. It is important to align the difference (that's the answer) with the subtrahend and minuend such that the decimal points match. This way, the decimal positions of the difference will match the decimal positions of the subtrahend and minuend. Remember to include the decimal point in your answer. Study the examples below and refer to them as needed to guide your practice – until you can solve the problems by yourself. When you complete a page of exercises, check your answers in the back of the book – and learn from any mistakes that you might have made.

EXAMPLES

$4.23 - 0.078 =$

$0.449 - 0.035 =$

$$\begin{array}{r} {\scriptstyle 1\ 1210} \\ 4.23\cancel{0} \\ -0.078 \\ \hline 4.152 \end{array}$$

$$\begin{array}{r} 0.449 \\ -0.035 \\ \hline 0.414 \end{array}$$

Note that 4.23 ends in the hundredths place, while 0.078 ends in the thousandths place. Adding a trailing zero to 4.23 turns it into 4.230. Now 4.230 and 0.078 match in final decimal position.

0.82 − 0.224 =   34.2 − 19 =   7909 − 4.9 =

8 − 0.2 =   8.3 − 1.3 =   500 − 0.13 =

276 − 0.84 =   0.02 − 0.008 =   69 − 9.9 =

597.7 − 0.004 =   4 − 3.13 =   736 − 6.96 =

51.4 − 0.006 =   6.91 − 5.5 =   444.4 − 42.8 =

58.09 − 0.04 =   2.12 − 0.005 =   92.4 − 0.006 =

Practice Arithmetic with Decimals Workbook

5.889 − 0.087 =		0.8 − 0.4 =		0.84 − 0.003 =

7.112 − 3.67 =		77 − 4.5 =		76 − 0.008 =

0.67 − 0.004 =		74 − 0.375 =		3.4 − 0.03 =

0.45 − 0.037 =		3 − 0.09 =		89 − 61.2 =

7500 − 50.7 =		7.3 − 4.802 =		859.9 − 0.03 =

323 − 87.9 =		40.81 − 0.661 =		93.51 − 0.021 =

3 − 0.3 =   5.83 − 0.07 =   191.4 − 34.2 =

2 − 0.006 =   19.5 − 6.38 =   42.32 − 0.033 =

92.1 − 0.55 =   291.2 − 14.5 =   260 − 0.005 =

4091 − 0.721 =   0.123 − 0.09 =   0.292 − 0.001 =

4.6 − 0.056 =   3 − 0.7 =   272.9 − 247.2 =

0.91 − 0.027 =   72 − 5.11 =   649.7 − 9.187 =

Practice Arithmetic with Decimals Workbook

94 − 0.002 =   5.11 − 1.921 =   5.43 − 0.02 =

6.74 − 0.654 =   3.705 − 2 =   5.47 − 0.071 =

6.7 − 6.012 =   3935 − 4.2 =   0.6 − 0.001 =

0.07 − 0.004 =   0.04 − 0.03 =   951 − 631.9 =

1.019 − 0.04 =   26 − 0.009 =   0.76 − 0.026 =

72.16 − 2 =   180 − 2.782 =   96.31 − 0.52 =

Improve Your Math Fluency Series

0.698 − 0.005 =   9.49 − 0.2 =   70 − 3.83 =

6.451 − 3.47 =   3.49 − 0.643 =   9.72 − 2.14 =

606.5 − 534 =   68 − 0.021 =   5.1 − 0.076 =

0.54 − 0.51 =   57.92 − 14 =   97 − 0.766 =

58 − 0.008 =   8854 − 42.5 =   58.51 − 32.27 =

34.8 − 12.72 =   321.5 − 0.004 =   6.836 − 3.9 =

Practice Arithmetic with Decimals Workbook

8.514 − 5 =		35.84 − 7.454 =		631.7 − 0.06 =

89 − 0.2 =		55 − 0.849 =		8.5 − 2.7 =

7.846 − 0.95 =		0.28 − 0.001 =		984 − 0.335 =

3232 − 19.6 =		92.95 − 5 =		84.57 − 58 =

9.2 − 0.005 =		4 − 0.331 =		4266 − 87.2 =

42.1 − 5.66 =		6.13 − 2 =		71.56 − 9 =

216 − 0.828 =   0.2 − 0.06 =   46 − 0.007 =

667.3 − 0.46 =   6.467 − 4 =   18.81 − 3.618 =

3.69 − 0.009 =   3.502 − 0.487 =   4.2 − 0.023 =

75.43 − 0.003 =   5 − 0.07 =   0.75 − 0.13 =

594 − 2.99 =   5.38 − 5 =   3 − 0.96 =

0.44 − 0.22 =   1463 − 42.5 =   5.125 − 0.94 =

Practice Arithmetic with Decimals Workbook

8029 − 512 =		32.58 − 0.008 =		4 − 0.001 =

51 − 7.796 =		56.5 − 51.75 =		798.4 − 58 =

725 − 0.098 =		3745 − 0.7 =		689.7 − 0.731 =

212.5 − 142.8 =		2.11 − 0.05 =		236.2 − 0.01 =

70.4 − 6.065 =		2 − 0.6 =		4.334 − 2.271 =

2.9 − 0.576 =		57.7 − 0.863 =		832.7 − 0.71 =

29.95 − 26.4 =	6866 − 0.67 =	0.089 − 0.005 =

906.8 − 2.64 =	846 − 0.9 =	20.13 − 16 =

78.49 − 44.23 =	698.1 − 0.831 =	8.61 − 5.102 =

76.68 − 0.004 =	29.5 − 18.9 =	2.92 − 0.04 =

3.84 − 3.21 =	31.68 − 0.654 =	0.056 − 0.004 =

4.9 − 2.1 =	7268 − 0.3 =	7.2 − 3 =

Practice Arithmetic with Decimals Workbook

527 − 0.36 =	0.7 − 0.006 =	16.2 − 0.659 =

71 − 4.13 =	8255 − 25.41 =	4 − 0.037 =

4.624 − 0.005 =	96.5 − 31.3 =	8.11 − 0.039 =

7.825 − 0.02 =	0.098 − 0.082 =	157.8 − 0.002 =

3.149 − 1.445 =	51.9 − 2 =	676 − 597 =

7487 − 0.095 =	927.3 − 8.8 =	8.6 − 0.087 =

Improve Your Math Fluency Series

99 − 0.953 =		9 − 4.3 =		1.7 − 0.2 =

68 − 0.51 =		2.985 − 0.54 =		2.049 − 0.049 =

321.3 − 0.05 =		69 − 4.89 =		902.8 − 0.7 =

5054 − 723.9 =		24.1 − 7.55 =		66 − 37.8 =

8 − 4 =			0.4 − 0.006 =		671 − 0.07 =

700 − 0.031 =		0.16 − 0.04 =		763 − 76.16 =

Practice Arithmetic with Decimals Workbook

$4 - 0.005 =$ $7 - 0.088 =$ $15.8 - 0.01 =$

$330 - 0.21 =$ $0.09 - 0.007 =$ $460 - 0.1 =$

$4.86 - 0.045 =$ $2770 - 35.3 =$ $1747 - 0.007 =$

$68.7 - 8 =$ $653 - 0.47 =$ $9.41 - 0.2 =$

$9097 - 0.852 =$ $352.6 - 0.014 =$ $93.3 - 50.4 =$

$0.8 - 0.002 =$ $380.1 - 5.81 =$ $3.99 - 0.75 =$

$16 - 0.026 =$　　　　$7.8 - 2.335 =$　　　　$6.3 - 0.048 =$

$7.1 - 2.56 =$　　　　$0.09 - 0.079 =$　　　　$446 - 0.967 =$

$660 - 255.6 =$　　　　$6.59 - 0.08 =$　　　　$49 - 0.006 =$

$14 - 0.018 =$　　　　$9.23 - 7.4 =$　　　　$0.09 - 0.009 =$

$57 - 0.19 =$　　　　$2128 - 582.2 =$　　　　$6.06 - 0.84 =$

$52 - 0.01 =$　　　　$868.3 - 0.2 =$　　　　$7.064 - 2 =$

Practice Arithmetic with Decimals Workbook

70.5 − 0.08 =   365 − 52.3 =   8 − 0.01 =

0.07 − 0.067 =   21.1 − 0.01 =   66.3 − 7 =

728 − 0.141 =   64 − 54.91 =   28.35 − 0.1 =

2.178 − 0.003 =   80 − 0.452 =   55 − 0.001 =

2294 − 9.2 =   6.99 − 0.06 =   262 − 0.879 =

6.22 − 1 =   27.5 − 0.58 =   502.4 − 10.23 =

Improve Your Math Fluency Series

7.8 − 0.06 =   9.6 − 0.05 =   0.089 − 0.064 =

87.26 − 0.22 =   11 − 9.937 =   554.2 − 93.37 =

9.88 − 0.5 =   36.1 − 4.7 =   524 − 0.4 =

1.5 − 0.024 =   77 − 0.97 =   0.9 − 0.53 =

14.65 − 0.2 =   1.8 − 0.63 =   12 − 0.004 =

69 − 57.5 =   232.3 − 9.73 =   4 − 2.93 =

Practice Arithmetic with Decimals Workbook

0.921 − 0.09 =		568 − 0.5 =		90.36 − 4 =

62 − 0.552 =		36.49 − 0.3 =		9 − 2.4 =

90.8 − 3.079 =		9 − 3.54 =		25.2 − 7.9 =

11.25 − 8 =		0.9 − 0.77 =		9.3 − 0.08 =

30.15 − 27.5 =		271 − 0.9 =		150.5 − 5.99 =

8574 − 7.75 =		1138 − 0.049 =		628 − 0.084 =

Improve Your Math Fluency Series

862.2 − 7.6 =   16 − 0.07 =   0.07 − 0.002 =

308 − 89 =   87.88 − 6.76 =   0.18 − 0.04 =

0.362 − 0.005 =   926 − 9 =   44.9 − 1.46 =

4.693 − 0.4 =   591.1 − 70.9 =   921.2 − 384.6 =

8.57 − 0.157 =   0.04 − 0.002 =   131 − 8.27 =

3866 − 14.6 =   5.829 − 4.3 =   82.47 − 3.397 =

Practice Arithmetic with Decimals Workbook

$0.112 - 0.073 =$ $21.98 - 0.1 =$ $7927 - 0.016 =$

$3.8 - 0.326 =$ $81 - 1.065 =$ $440 - 6.57 =$

$1 - 0.3 =$ $1.19 - 0.2 =$ $5.1 - 0.16 =$

$1687 - 0.834 =$ $0.1 - 0.09 =$ $0.944 - 0.001 =$

$0.41 - 0.097 =$ $5 - 0.74 =$ $9.6 - 0.9 =$

$429.1 - 0.008 =$ $482 - 5.046 =$ $7 - 1.6 =$

Improve Your Math Fluency Series

73.76 − 0.4 =   0.59 − 0.009 =   9 − 0.8 =

2676 − 0.108 =   843 − 12.97 =   6741 − 0.51 =

5.324 − 4.92 =   6 − 0.005 =   167.8 − 89 =

486 − 6.29 =   0.237 − 0.093 =   390.9 − 51 =

3.34 − 0.707 =   799.6 − 4.65 =   7.415 − 0.057 =

0.9 − 0.6 =   34.9 − 0.38 =   7849 − 649.2 =

Practice Arithmetic with Decimals Workbook

12.9 − 0.6 =   5.1 − 0.41 =   885 − 2.64 =

727 − 42.4 =   43 − 0.012 =   421.8 − 9.8 =

98 − 0.03 =   72 − 0.094 =   872.1 − 0.94 =

424 − 2.15 =   207.6 − 87.6 =   7.58 − 4 =

91.44 − 7 =   619 − 0.637 =   88.6 − 42.3 =

2.52 − 0.004 =   1906 − 0.1 =   0.72 − 0.6 =

47

Part 3: Practice Multiplying Numbers with Decimals

To multiply numbers with decimals, stack them vertically. Unlike adding and subtracting numbers with decimals, align the factors (the two numbers that you are multiplying together) by their rightmost digits (not by the decimal point). Don't worry if the decimal places don't match – as long as the rightmost digits are aligned. Then multiply the numbers the same way that you would multiply whole numbers. Align the intermediate numbers by the rightmost digit the same way that you would ordinarily align them if you were multiplying whole numbers together. Lastly, you need to determine where to put the decimal point in the product (that's the final answer). Count the number of digits in each factor that are to the right of their decimal points. Add these two numbers together. Place the decimal point of the product such that the number of digits to the right of its decimal point equals the sum of the numbers of digits to the right of the factors' decimal points. You may need to add leading zeroes to make this possible.

EXAMPLES

$4.23 \times 0.078 =$

$$
\begin{array}{r}
12 \\
12 \\
4.23 \\
\times\ 0.078 \\
\hline
0.03384 \\
0.29610 \\
\hline
0.32994
\end{array}
$$

$0.002 \times 0.5 =$

$$
\begin{array}{r}
0.002 \\
\times\ 0.5 \\
\hline
0.0010
\end{array}
$$

In the first example, the factor 4.23 has 2 digits to the right of its decimal point and the factor 0.078 has 3 digits to the right of its decimal point. Therefore, the product, 0.32994, has 5 digits to the right of its decimal point. That's how you determine where to put the decimal point in the answer. In the second example, the 0.002 has 3 digits to the right of its decimal point and 0.5 has 1 digit to the right of its decimal point. The answer, 0.0010, must then have 4 digits to the right of its decimal point. Notice that two leading zeroes had to be added (after the decimal point) in order to achieve this. Trailing zeroes of numbers with decimal points may be removed. For example, the answer 0.0010 may also be expressed as 0.001.

Practice Arithmetic with Decimals Workbook

$15.47 \times 0.005 =$ $8.08 \times 0.08 =$ $30 \times 14.4 =$

$0.006 \times 0.01 =$ $0.73 \times 2.8 =$ $910 \times 2.6 =$

$0.76 \times 2.9 =$ $0.705 \times 0.008 =$ $0.06 \times 71.6 =$

$306 \times 0.741 =$ $2.99 \times 7.4 =$ $896.8 \times 0.08 =$

9.2 × 0.06 =   30.49 × 7050 =   0.62 × 644 =

70 × 7.2 =   4.6 × 689.6 =   9.77 × 40 =

0.52 × 1.739 =   0.944 × 2 =   0.005 × 8.673 =

0.91 × 1.3 =   90.3 × 93 =   71.37 × 973.5 =

Practice Arithmetic with Decimals Workbook

0.046 × 375 =	321 × 0.008 =	5.62 × 5.1 =

364.1 × 910.2 =	0.33 × 0.092 =	6.48 × 3 =

3.8 × 0.695 =	4738 × 4.312 =	20 × 0.236 =

0.007 × 1 =	10.7 × 0.084 =	0.02 × 29 =

0.052 × 34.5 =   94.5 × 55 =   46.7 × 1.137 =

0.02 × 0.07 =   0.8 × 710 =   7.214 × 1534 =

0.6 × 3491 =   0.025 × 8.6 =   46.9 × 0.04 =

0.2 × 0.53 =   0.9 × 0.04 =   8 × 5.809 =

Practice Arithmetic with Decimals Workbook

$3.2 \times 99.7 =$ $35.4 \times 97.9 =$ $3694 \times 0.9 =$

$0.371 \times 0.71 =$ $22.22 \times 1.92 =$ $71.1 \times 1.278 =$

$82 \times 0.81 =$ $70 \times 0.037 =$ $42.32 \times 21 =$

$2810 \times 55.1 =$ $0.05 \times 42 =$ $5 \times 0.007 =$

30.4 × 70.2 =   77 × 3.19 =   0.615 × 0.824 =

50.25 × 5.84 =   0.07 × 6 =   0.231 × 6.202 =

9.07 × 112.9 =   44 × 0.04 =   655.2 × 3.7 =

9.59 × 0.003 =   0.12 × 8.8 =   15 × 0.074 =

Practice Arithmetic with Decimals Workbook

2 × 0.62 =					0.08 × 14 =					49.9 × 959.2 =

0.052 × 61 =				559 × 8.075 =				3077 × 8 =

0.088 × 0.8 =				2.79 × 82.39 =				4.734 × 0.007 =

0.65 × 0.009 =				0.01 × 71.28 =				0.08 × 0.85 =

Improve Your Math Fluency Series

0.6 × 768 =	0.8 × 65.12 =	0.086 × 0.2 =

1 × 0.6 =	0.003 × 0.2 =	9.62 × 0.007 =

0.94 × 0.7 =	0.1 × 24.5 =	2.11 × 92 =

0.2 × 379 =	641.5 × 137.9 =	0.05 × 91.27 =

Practice Arithmetic with Decimals Workbook

86.3 × 0.8 =				10 × 4.815 =				94 × 0.085 =

40.07 × 2.902 =			53.5 × 0.02 =				2.6 × 0.021 =

0.4 × 0.865 =				9 × 0.09 =				0.9 × 0.43 =

0.751 × 96 =				0.047 × 319 =				7.42 × 0.3 =

$8655 \times 0.002 =$ $\qquad$ $80.3 \times 0.3 =$ $\qquad$ $9362 \times 8.689 =$

$0.008 \times 954 =$ $\qquad$ $5 \times 0.369 =$ $\qquad$ $6 \times 274.6 =$

$0.095 \times 0.1 =$ $\qquad$ $13.84 \times 893 =$ $\qquad$ $5 \times 0.81 =$

$8.483 \times 267.7 =$ $\qquad$ $3581 \times 0.004 =$ $\qquad$ $82.41 \times 239.8 =$

Practice Arithmetic with Decimals Workbook

79.93 × 6 =		2.68 × 0.881 =		34 × 0.39 =

0.04 × 44.9 =		10.46 × 0.07 =		865.3 × 0.663 =

63.6 × 0.49 =		6.1 × 1.479 =		0.805 × 9 =

0.007 × 4670 =		780.7 × 8 =		0.9 × 34 =

9494 × 8.3 =   68.5 × 25.36 =   39 × 69.55 =

63.2 × 64 =   7 × 1.374 =   7.37 × 247 =

0.285 × 0.4 =   4 × 637.6 =   10.73 × 95 =

0.73 × 91.85 =   90.9 × 6.339 =   0.7 × 0.3 =

Practice Arithmetic with Decimals Workbook

500 × 0.4 =		0.019 × 410 =		392.8 × 72.09 =

2 × 0.461 =		58 × 3.011 =		0.03 × 67.12 =

96.59 × 7 =		614 × 0.75 =		0.9 × 63.4 =

0.7 × 1.517 =		0.382 × 3.7 =		0.089 × 19 =

0.83 × 6.64 =   0.2 × 0.024 =   22.4 × 0.5 =

6 × 2 =   0.24 × 0.004 =   0.06 × 0.9 =

0.5 × 0.01 =   345 × 5.8 =   4 × 0.03 =

0.012 × 0.046 =   0.027 × 1.384 =   0.09 × 59.2 =

Practice Arithmetic with Decimals Workbook

4292 × 8.59 =   660.6 × 77 =   959.6 × 1.95 =

0.79 × 74.74 =   50 × 82.3 =   772.1 × 9.92 =

0.01 × 7.762 =   0.002 × 4084 =   5 × 22.98 =

0.98 × 9.4 =   4.8 × 75.4 =   46.1 × 0.03 =

63

0.002 × 28 =	7.3 × 8.94 =	230.2 × 0.005 =

5 × 0.08 =	0.787 × 4.501 =	0.04 × 0.003 =

66.96 × 2.8 =	5.302 × 6.09 =	909.9 × 4242 =

5598 × 4.2 =	0.001 × 3.4 =	1.33 × 0.736 =

Practice Arithmetic with Decimals Workbook

3.66 × 34 =   54 × 0.7 =   0.1 × 19.23 =

240.5 × 1.962 =   0.003 × 0.002 =   0.003 × 0.058 =

188 × 59.7 =   822.3 × 701.8 =   0.04 × 6 =

69 × 0.69 =   0.032 × 163.5 =   3 × 9.002 =

0.09 × 2.16 =   0.7 × 4 =   60 × 0.7 =

0.69 × 25.27 =   13.7 × 736.9 =   0.045 × 0.007 =

7.35 × 0.5 =   0.03 × 0.64 =   2.4 × 290.9 =

8.1 × 9 =   0.009 × 6 =   2.876 × 2.92 =

Practice Arithmetic with Decimals Workbook

2.4 × 154 =		9.72 × 1 =		0.18 × 0.8 =

0.07 × 2.771 =		2 × 0.49 =		2 × 5.191 =

2446 × 0.3 =		635 × 4.7 =		0.023 × 0.3 =

0.071 × 7412 =		0.6 × 4317 =		0.07 × 0.02 =

0.63 × 3.14 =   3684 × 738.2 =   5 × 0.004 =

0.32 × 2 =   241 × 99 =   68.42 × 5.24 =

87.2 × 0.217 =   5 × 724.1 =   968.8 × 45.5 =

2.7 × 996.4 =   683 × 0.02 =   25 × 0.043 =

Part 4: Practice Long Division with Decimals – Level I

To divide numbers with decimals, arrange them in long division form just as you would if you were dividing whole numbers. Then divide the numbers the same way that you would divide whole numbers. However, instead of writing a remainder, add trailing zeroes to the dividend (that's the number you are dividing into) as needed. The decimal position of the quotient (the final answer) comes about quite naturally. That is, as you carry out the long division, you multiply digits of the quotient (the answer above the dividend) with the divisor (that's the number you are dividing by, which appears at the left). You'll have to put the decimal position in the right place (using the rule for multiplying numbers with decimals) in the quotient to make this work.

Long division with decimals is divided into two levels in this workbook. You won't need to worry about repeating decimals until Part 5 (which are described in the introduction to Part 5). Study the examples below and refer to them as needed to guide your practice – until you can solve the problems by yourself. When you complete a page of exercises, check your answers in the back of the book – and learn from any mistakes that you might have made.

EXAMPLES

$0.448 \div 1.4$ $\qquad$ $0.4 \div 0.16$

$$
\begin{array}{r}
0.32 \\
1.4 \overline{\smash{)}0.448} \\
\underline{0.42} \\
0.028 \\
\underline{0.028} \\
0
\end{array}
\qquad
\begin{array}{r}
2.5 \\
0.16 \overline{\smash{)}0.40} \\
\underline{0.32} \\
0.08 \\
\underline{0.08} \\
0
\end{array}
$$

Notice that 0.4 divided by 0.16 would have had a remainder, but by adding the trailing zero to 0.4 to turn it into 0.40, the answer could be expressed as a decimal rather than with a remainder. In fact, all remainder problems of whole number long division can be expressed in decimal form. For example, 25 divided by 4, which would normally be 6 with a remainder of 1, is found to be 6.25 using the method of long division with decimals. Try it!

$4.2 \overline{)35.28}$ $2.8 \overline{)103.6}$ $0.5 \overline{)35.5}$

$14 \overline{)122.78}$ $1.6 \overline{)0.112}$ $0.6 \overline{)0.54}$

$0.1 \overline{)0.006}$ $8 \overline{)60.8}$ $7 \overline{)5.25}$

$0.8 \overline{)61.28}$ $5 \overline{)1.5}$ $1 \overline{)0.93}$

Practice Arithmetic with Decimals Workbook

7.3) 51.1   84) 20.16   0.8) 4.8

91) 787.15   1) 3.3   6) 3.6

1.3) 32.63   0.4) 0.24   8) 27.2

0.5) 4.5   0.2) 0.04   0.2) 0.002

$9.1 \overline{)4167.8}$ $52 \overline{)2.08}$ $0.7 \overline{)28.7}$

$7 \overline{)9.03}$ $8 \overline{)3.2}$ $0.6 \overline{)4.2}$

$0.41 \overline{)8.61}$ $5.5 \overline{)49.5}$ $8.6 \overline{)15.05}$

$0.2 \overline{)1.2}$ $1 \overline{)61.2}$ $0.7 \overline{)0.21}$

Practice Arithmetic with Decimals Workbook

$0.3 \overline{)0.57}$ $2.9 \overline{)0.087}$ $0.3 \overline{)0.06}$

$14 \overline{)0.7}$ $8.1 \overline{)356.4}$ $0.3 \overline{)0.21}$

$3.7 \overline{)6.364}$ $4 \overline{)1.84}$ $4 \overline{)355.2}$

$9.2 \overline{)55.2}$ $1 \overline{)0.08}$ $9.8 \overline{)0.49}$

$18 \overline{)19.8}$ $7 \overline{)0.42}$ $9.2 \overline{)7884.4}$

$3.7 \overline{)2.146}$ $0.045 \overline{)3.924}$ $0.3 \overline{)0.006}$

$1 \overline{)0.3}$ $9 \overline{)64.8}$ $5.4 \overline{)443.34}$

$0.6 \overline{)5.172}$ $0.5 \overline{)0.005}$ $5.2 \overline{)379.6}$

Practice Arithmetic with Decimals Workbook

$0.7 \overline{) 0.217}$ $0.3 \overline{) 0.009}$ $0.1 \overline{) 0.52}$

$27 \overline{) 1.35}$ $0.9 \overline{) 0.27}$ $5.1 \overline{) 5.1}$

$0.1 \overline{) 8.48}$ $0.078 \overline{) 0.624}$ $0.1 \overline{) 68.4}$

$6.8 \overline{) 67.864}$ $36 \overline{) 338.4}$ $0.1 \overline{) 1.93}$

$0.2 \overline{) 0.78}$ $\qquad$ $1.1 \overline{) 2.53}$ $\qquad$ $7 \overline{) 16.8}$

$4.4 \overline{) 13.64}$ $\qquad$ $18 \overline{) 0.9}$ $\qquad$ $9 \overline{) 680.4}$

$79 \overline{) 31.6}$ $\qquad$ $5 \overline{) 0.2}$ $\qquad$ $0.088 \overline{) 5.896}$

$4.8 \overline{) 41.52}$ $\qquad$ $89 \overline{) 2.67}$ $\qquad$ $68 \overline{) 0.68}$

Practice Arithmetic with Decimals Workbook

$0.1 \overline{) 0.004}$ $\qquad$ $0.4 \overline{) 1.088}$ $\qquad$ $0.8 \overline{) 3.2}$

$7 \overline{) 66.5}$ $\qquad$ $0.01 \overline{) 0.039}$ $\qquad$ $4.1 \overline{) 3.28}$

$8.8 \overline{) 2164.8}$ $\qquad$ $55 \overline{) 93.5}$ $\qquad$ $3 \overline{) 11.1}$

$9.8 \overline{) 839.86}$ $\qquad$ $0.3 \overline{) 0.03}$ $\qquad$ $2 \overline{) 1.86}$

$0.9 \overline{)4.5}$ $\qquad$ $0.4 \overline{)29.6}$ $\qquad$ $2 \overline{)2.18}$

$0.8 \overline{)0.048}$ $\qquad$ $7.8 \overline{)226.2}$ $\qquad$ $17 \overline{)8.5}$

$7 \overline{)31.5}$ $\qquad$ $99 \overline{)237.6}$ $\qquad$ $0.8 \overline{)6.24}$

$0.8 \overline{)481.6}$ $\qquad$ $8 \overline{)3.2}$ $\qquad$ $1.4 \overline{)12.6}$

Practice Arithmetic with Decimals Workbook

$0.8 \overline{)78.4}$ $0.4 \overline{)0.8}$ $8.3 \overline{)805.1}$

$33 \overline{)1.32}$ $44 \overline{)180.4}$ $0.8 \overline{)7.76}$

$91 \overline{)5.46}$ $0.8 \overline{)68.72}$ $0.8 \overline{)0.232}$

$8 \overline{)72.32}$ $61 \overline{)3.05}$ $9 \overline{)80.1}$

$0.6 \overline{) 0.036}$ $9 \overline{) 3.6}$ $53 \overline{) 3.18}$

$36 \overline{) 154.8}$ $0.8 \overline{) 2.488}$ $9.4 \overline{) 4042}$

$0.9 \overline{) 0.054}$ $2.7 \overline{) 108}$ $2 \overline{) 0.14}$

$5.1 \overline{) 17.34}$ $0.3 \overline{) 11.1}$ $0.1 \overline{) 8.68}$

Practice Arithmetic with Decimals Workbook

$0.1 \overline{)0.039}$ $0.6 \overline{)0.24}$ $0.9 \overline{)2.34}$

$58 \overline{)46.4}$ $0.5 \overline{)0.02}$ $78 \overline{)631.8}$

$4.7 \overline{)0.893}$ $28 \overline{)212.8}$ $6 \overline{)55.32}$

$0.4 \overline{)0.4}$ $0.3 \overline{)296.4}$ $2 \overline{)0.08}$

$0.76 \overline{) 38.76}$ $\qquad$ $0.4 \overline{) 0.236}$ $\qquad$ $0.2 \overline{) 0.58}$

$0.8 \overline{) 0.016}$ $\qquad$ $0.6 \overline{) 5.88}$ $\qquad$ $51 \overline{) 27.03}$

$8 \overline{) 69.6}$ $\qquad$ $1 \overline{) 3.6}$ $\qquad$ $4.8 \overline{) 4752}$

$0.3 \overline{) 0.021}$ $\qquad$ $9.3 \overline{) 0.93}$ $\qquad$ $2.9 \overline{) 0.986}$

Practice Arithmetic with Decimals Workbook

2.6) 0.26   36) 176.4   0.9) 7.2

0.5) 1   89) 5509.1   0.7) 0.217

8.5) 25.5   0.3) 0.069   4) 3.2

0.8) 0.32   0.2) 4   5) 0.75

$48 \overline{) 1329.6}$ $3.9 \overline{) 330.72}$ $98 \overline{) 97.02}$

$7 \overline{) 60.2}$ $9 \overline{) 0.63}$ $0.7 \overline{) 0.07}$

$0.1 \overline{) 0.7}$ $1.9 \overline{) 55.1}$ $3 \overline{) 2.22}$

$0.9 \overline{) 0.36}$ $0.06 \overline{) 0.048}$ $0.3 \overline{) 17.4}$

Practice Arithmetic with Decimals Workbook

$0.5 \overline{) 229.5}$ $0.4 \overline{) 1.2}$ $0.8 \overline{) 0.56}$

$0.6 \overline{) 0.576}$ $0.005 \overline{) 0.013}$ $3.2 \overline{) 1.6}$

$3.2 \overline{) 27.2}$ $0.2 \overline{) 0.026}$ $0.6 \overline{) 0.048}$

$99 \overline{) 68.31}$ $73 \overline{) 483.26}$ $0.4 \overline{) 28.08}$

$0.9 \overline{)0.666}$ $4 \overline{)2.4}$ $8.8 \overline{)3.52}$

$68 \overline{)5698.4}$ $7.3 \overline{)2.92}$ $0.7 \overline{)4.9}$

$7.5 \overline{)264}$ $2 \overline{)17.6}$ $7 \overline{)0.28}$

$0.2 \overline{)1.866}$ $5.1 \overline{)40.749}$ $0.22 \overline{)0.11}$

Practice Arithmetic with Decimals Workbook

5.5) 16.5   67) 22.78   8) 0.32

5) 31.75   0.8) 23.12   4) 0.2

2.3) 48.3   7.3) 1.46   5.5) 52.8

0.4) 0.132   7.5) 5.25   9.9) 9.801

3.6) 0.216   8.7) 6.003   0.3) 0.012

5.2) 2.964   1.8) 0.054   0.4) 1.932

0.3) 24.6   3.1) 21.7   89) 380.92

1.8) 0.18   2) 7.6   0.1) 0.09

Practice Arithmetic with Decimals Workbook

$0.1 \overline{) 0.064}$ $4.9 \overline{) 3944.5}$ $72 \overline{) 518.4}$

$10 \overline{) 0.3}$ $0.2 \overline{) 167.8}$ $23 \overline{) 20.7}$

$6.9 \overline{) 55.2}$ $0.5 \overline{) 23.4}$ $9 \overline{) 50.4}$

$0.9 \overline{) 6.75}$ $6 \overline{) 0.24}$ $2 \overline{) 15.6}$

Part 5: Practice Long Division with Decimals – Level II

Sometimes, the method of long division with numbers with decimals never ends! That is, you need to keep adding trailing zeroes to the dividend forever. Fortunately, when this happens the digits repeat in a pattern. This is called a repeating decimal. For example, 1 divided by 3 results in 0.3333... Try it and see for yourself. The digit 3 repeats forever. This repeating decimal is denoted by adding a bar over it: $0.\overline{3}$. The $\overline{3}$ represents an infinite sequence of 3's. So $0.\overline{3}$ is actually larger than 0.3. Similarly, 11 divided by 9 equals $1.\overline{2}$. Try it yourself.

You might get a repeating sequence of digits rather than a single repeating digit. For example, 20 divided by 11 equals $1.\overline{81}$. Try it and see. In this case, the 81 sequence repeats over and over. That is, $1.\overline{81}$ represents 1.818181... The 81 repeats forever. The sequence may be long. For example, 3 divided by 7 equals $0.\overline{428571}$.

Some, but not all, of the answers in Part 5 involve repeating decimals. If the decimal sequence has not started to repeat by the 9th decimal position, the answer (in the back of the book) has been rounded to the nearest billionth. However, it would be reasonable for the student to carry the answers out only to a handful of significant figures. Study the examples below and refer to them as needed to guide your practice – until you can solve the problems by yourself. When you complete a page of exercises, check your answers in the back of the book – and learn from any mistakes that you might have made.

EXAMPLES

$0.337 \div 1.8$

$0.05 \div 0.6$

$0.08\overline{3}$
$0.6 \overline{)0.0500}$
$\underline{0.048}$
0.0020
$\underline{0.0018}$
0.00020

$0.187\overline{2}$
$1.8 \overline{)0.337}$
$\underline{0.18}$
0.157
$\underline{0.144}$
0.0130
$\underline{0.0126}$
0.00040
$\underline{0.00036}$
0.000040

Notice that the 20 and 40 repeat at the end of these examples. This is how you know if and when the decimal is repeating.

Practice Arithmetic with Decimals Workbook

$4.9 \overline{) 1.5}$ $4.7 \overline{) 3}$ $0.8 \overline{) 0.5}$

$0.7 \overline{) 6.86}$ $0.9 \overline{) 3.5}$ $0.1 \overline{) 7.6}$

$86 \overline{) 1.68}$ $1.1 \overline{) 0.91}$ $73 \overline{) 40.4}$

$10 \overline{) 0.7}$ $1.4 \overline{) 31}$ $4.2 \overline{) 3.7}$

$2 \overline{)8.6}$ $\qquad$ $1.2 \overline{)6}$ $\qquad$ $4 \overline{)3.88}$

$48 \overline{)0.02}$ $\qquad$ $4.9 \overline{)0.26}$ $\qquad$ $3 \overline{)8.9}$

$0.7 \overline{)4}$ $\qquad$ $1.4 \overline{)7.7}$ $\qquad$ $0.8 \overline{)2.47}$

$9.1 \overline{)2}$ $\qquad$ $1.6 \overline{)580}$ $\qquad$ $6 \overline{)0.95}$

Practice Arithmetic with Decimals Workbook

$0.7 \overline{)6.98}$ $7.8 \overline{)6}$ $91 \overline{)7.11}$

$5.1 \overline{)0.89}$ $3 \overline{)0.91}$ $8.8 \overline{)0.2}$

$3 \overline{)58.3}$ $3.6 \overline{)8.62}$ $0.2 \overline{)0.81}$

$7.1 \overline{)390}$ $8 \overline{)0.42}$ $2 \overline{)0.4}$

Improve Your Math Fluency Series

4.1) 9.64   0.5) 0.1   6.5) 0.3

5.8) 0.9   13) 1.6   8) 0.09

0.5) 0.28   3) 9.6   3.5) 318

1) 78.8   2.3) 6   0.8) 2.8

Practice Arithmetic with Decimals Workbook

$0.2 \overline{)6.2}$ $4 \overline{)95.9}$ $0.5 \overline{)7.2}$

$3.3 \overline{)1.2}$ $9 \overline{)9.2}$ $3.8 \overline{)7}$

$0.1 \overline{)0.8}$ $2 \overline{)0.08}$ $0.9 \overline{)0.02}$

$0.8 \overline{)3.2}$ $5.9 \overline{)0.01}$ $7.6 \overline{)4.1}$

$0.5 \overline{)0.59}$ $\qquad$ $0.2 \overline{)0.1}$ $\qquad$ $8.5 \overline{)9.1}$

$91 \overline{)0.47}$ $\qquad$ $0.4 \overline{)0.1}$ $\qquad$ $0.4 \overline{)0.9}$

$99 \overline{)0.06}$ $\qquad$ $9.3 \overline{)0.99}$ $\qquad$ $4.9 \overline{)18}$

$6 \overline{)0.9}$ $\qquad$ $8.5 \overline{)42.6}$ $\qquad$ $5 \overline{)0.52}$

Practice Arithmetic with Decimals Workbook

$41 \overline{) 0.05}$ $0.6 \overline{) 1.9}$ $8.3 \overline{) 0.7}$

$0.2 \overline{) 7.6}$ $89 \overline{) 0.7}$ $71 \overline{) 0.01}$

$4.9 \overline{) 546}$ $5.1 \overline{) 0.6}$ $0.1 \overline{) 24}$

$16 \overline{) 3.7}$ $0.9 \overline{) 1.08}$ $98 \overline{) 0.18}$

$9.6 \overline{) 0.2}$ $\qquad$ $8 \overline{) 0.69}$ $\qquad$ $1 \overline{) 7.2}$

$19 \overline{) 0.87}$ $\qquad$ $8.7 \overline{) 0.3}$ $\qquad$ $6.3 \overline{) 0.07}$

$0.4 \overline{) 3.8}$ $\qquad$ $0.9 \overline{) 9.4}$ $\qquad$ $0.3 \overline{) 0.62}$

$2.1 \overline{) 280}$ $\qquad$ $57 \overline{) 7.5}$ $\qquad$ $0.9 \overline{) 631}$

Practice Arithmetic with Decimals Workbook

$8.5 \overline{)0.4}$ $\quad\quad\quad$ $8.3 \overline{)4.3}$ $\quad\quad\quad$ $7.4 \overline{)462}$

$0.7 \overline{)0.39}$ $\quad\quad\quad$ $4.2 \overline{)0.09}$ $\quad\quad\quad$ $6 \overline{)0.8}$

$1.2 \overline{)0.64}$ $\quad\quad\quad$ $0.9 \overline{)0.5}$ $\quad\quad\quad$ $0.5 \overline{)0.94}$

$7 \overline{)7.96}$ $\quad\quad\quad$ $2 \overline{)0.67}$ $\quad\quad\quad$ $1.6 \overline{)0.03}$

$0.1 \overline{) 0.7}$ $\qquad$ $0.8 \overline{) 3}$ $\qquad$ $5.2 \overline{) 0.02}$

$36 \overline{) 0.5}$ $\qquad$ $0.8 \overline{) 1}$ $\qquad$ $22 \overline{) 0.69}$

$3 \overline{) 49.2}$ $\qquad$ $4.6 \overline{) 0.9}$ $\qquad$ $59 \overline{) 0.81}$

$59 \overline{) 0.22}$ $\qquad$ $6 \overline{) 0.3}$ $\qquad$ $4.4 \overline{) 44.3}$

Practice Arithmetic with Decimals Workbook

$4.9 \overline{)85}$ $\qquad$ $9.4 \overline{)8.4}$ $\qquad$ $10 \overline{)0.02}$

$0.6 \overline{)4}$ $\qquad$ $4 \overline{)5.48}$ $\qquad$ $9.7 \overline{)0.55}$

$4.6 \overline{)0.35}$ $\qquad$ $7 \overline{)9.6}$ $\qquad$ $0.9 \overline{)95}$

$6.1 \overline{)216}$ $\qquad$ $7 \overline{)5.6}$ $\qquad$ $92 \overline{)5.1}$

$42 \overline{)0.1}$ $\qquad$ $1 \overline{)9.32}$ $\qquad$ $7.2 \overline{)0.6}$

$57 \overline{)0.6}$ $\qquad$ $0.9 \overline{)63.1}$ $\qquad$ $4.5 \overline{)0.13}$

$0.9 \overline{)0.5}$ $\qquad$ $1 \overline{)19.5}$ $\qquad$ $0.008 \overline{)0.089}$

$0.2 \overline{)1.34}$ $\qquad$ $0.2 \overline{)0.09}$ $\qquad$ $2 \overline{)97.2}$

Practice Arithmetic with Decimals Workbook

$0.3 \overline{)312}$ $\quad\quad$ $0.5 \overline{)4}$ $\quad\quad$ $2.6 \overline{)5.7}$

$8.9 \overline{)8.9}$ $\quad\quad$ $0.1 \overline{)0.93}$ $\quad\quad$ $1.2 \overline{)0.05}$

$3 \overline{)0.06}$ $\quad\quad$ $3.5 \overline{)138}$ $\quad\quad$ $9.9 \overline{)56.9}$

$28 \overline{)0.25}$ $\quad\quad$ $5 \overline{)0.05}$ $\quad\quad$ $19 \overline{)3.83}$

Improve Your Math Fluency Series

$3.4 \overline{)9}$ $\qquad$ $2.7 \overline{)522}$ $\qquad$ $0.1 \overline{)579}$

$0.7 \overline{)4.2}$ $\qquad$ $0.5 \overline{)0.26}$ $\qquad$ $0.7 \overline{)7.83}$

$42 \overline{)45.4}$ $\qquad$ $0.9 \overline{)0.9}$ $\qquad$ $8.8 \overline{)69.2}$

$0.7 \overline{)0.4}$ $\qquad$ $40 \overline{)2.72}$ $\qquad$ $7 \overline{)0.3}$

Practice Arithmetic with Decimals Workbook

$0.6 \overline{)7}$ $93 \overline{)7.4}$ $0.1 \overline{)19}$

$5.6 \overline{)3.97}$ $0.5 \overline{)9.82}$ $3.2 \overline{)0.09}$

$0.5 \overline{)7.1}$ $97 \overline{)0.03}$ $82 \overline{)3.58}$

$0.8 \overline{)3.4}$ $0.003 \overline{)0.003}$ $9 \overline{)4.85}$

$5 \overline{)66.5}$ $9 \overline{)0.4}$ $0.8 \overline{)0.5}$

$5.6 \overline{)6.8}$ $5.8 \overline{)0.6}$ $3 \overline{)3.33}$

$1 \overline{)9.52}$ $58 \overline{)0.94}$ $7.7 \overline{)9}$

$0.4 \overline{)0.08}$ $82 \overline{)0.61}$ $73 \overline{)2.56}$

Practice Arithmetic with Decimals Workbook

$8.9 \overline{)9}$ $\qquad$ $0.7 \overline{)8.36}$ $\qquad$ $7 \overline{)5.39}$

$4 \overline{)0.16}$ $\qquad$ $42 \overline{)0.34}$ $\qquad$ $96 \overline{)1.9}$

$5 \overline{)0.3}$ $\qquad$ $32 \overline{)52.5}$ $\qquad$ $2 \overline{)2.22}$

$60 \overline{)0.3}$ $\qquad$ $6 \overline{)0.6}$ $\qquad$ $8.3 \overline{)5.77}$

$2 \overline{)5.08}$ $2.8 \overline{)0.95}$ $0.6 \overline{)1}$

$9 \overline{)0.9}$ $0.9 \overline{)0.5}$ $6.9 \overline{)0.86}$

$8.7 \overline{)7.17}$ $0.3 \overline{)87}$ $0.4 \overline{)691}$

$0.9 \overline{)9.1}$ $7.5 \overline{)571}$ $90 \overline{)0.09}$

Practice Arithmetic with Decimals Workbook

$19 \overline{)86.9}$ $2 \overline{)0.3}$ $8 \overline{)34.3}$

$0.5 \overline{)2}$ $0.7 \overline{)0.07}$ $73 \overline{)51.5}$

$50 \overline{)61.9}$ $4 \overline{)0.7}$ $6 \overline{)5.1}$

$0.6 \overline{)41.9}$ $0.4 \overline{)0.13}$ $90 \overline{)9.3}$

$6 \overline{)49.4}$　　　　$5.5 \overline{)27}$　　　　$35 \overline{)5.9}$

$0.08 \overline{)0.89}$　　　$1.9 \overline{)68.1}$　　　$46 \overline{)0.7}$

$58 \overline{)0.2}$　　　　$7.6 \overline{)0.4}$　　　　$0.6 \overline{)0.08}$

$81 \overline{)4.9}$　　　　$3.5 \overline{)0.8}$　　　　$1.8 \overline{)0.7}$

Answer Key

Part 1 Answers:

Page 7
42.9, 81.019, 32.7
76.675, 49.414, 7.9
64.327, 996.8, 1009.8
45.06, 987.3, 50.512
0.096, 407.2, 128
7.9, 92.239, 58.149

Page 8
0.19, 1.202, 3.19
2.968, 33.67, 854.1
0.311, 2396.058, 92.09
3.02, 451.9, 46.166
900.8, 14.283, 2.027
2597.5, 78.4, 8.931

Page 9
30.853, 97.061, 165.28
16.508, 869.79, 0.909
1.427, 19.6, 4.49
459.8, 93.4, 6214.7
60.16, 23.22, 24.769
9.176, 4.601, 7.841

Page 10
3.075, 0.678, 6.001
2.302, 7618.89, 6008.077
0.105, 76.49, 3.45
69.01, 2.008, 32.82
2527.505, 101.8, 12.119
785.084, 1.72, 1621

Page 11
2.206, 520.438, 0.115
9.056, 870.9, 2.866
4.129, 7.17, 57.06
619.004, 34.5, 542.091
6.39, 7.004, 1.01
501.81, 4349.75, 649.38

Page 12
37.083, 10.351, 15.35
6.896, 4.108, 3.982
88.55, 7.622, 7.925
9.553, 66.1, 0.17
28, 2306, 31.62
22.04, 84.3, 6.176

Page 13
33.8, 0.057, 752.979
162.6, 9.697, 522.3
61.463, 410.804, 25.8
585.69, 345.915, 89.4
496.635, 705.6, 422.48
808.255, 8.79, 5594.28

Page 14
774.703, 314.12, 34.657
5.17, 3820.001, 9739.8
0.343, 1.7, 104.02
154.8, 2.633, 65.91
90.67, 31.11, 3.9
99.06, 867.869, 0.47

Page 15
222.36, 9010.4, 3221.2
0.986, 216.001, 15.3
3.439, 32.43, 11.15
738.2, 0.295, 8360.24
1.76, 74.1, 777.18
5.006, 6441.07, 82.59

Page 16
5968.6, 0.053, 73.56
42.28, 887.103, 6.333
577.2, 8.54, 14.02
17.815, 313.044, 0.073
863.038, 44.64, 5813.5
7245.94, 2.403, 97

111

Page 17
43.2, 0.628, 709.8
744.63, 1.05, 7073.9
9.204, 0.88, 891.57
535.54, 4.69, 7.195
958.5, 9396.895, 43.9
0.955, 239.3, 36.93

Page 18
17.07, 642.8, 11.802
4.86, 6081.018, 94.09
8.21, 62.75, 2.7
379.5, 0.935, 0.99
93.6, 9.642, 1.804
3.039, 396.92, 97.93

Page 19
987.007, 62.828, 83.63
97, 81.327, 73.4
3.912, 1129.7, 63.306
2.964, 0.24, 86.6
217.8, 1, 40.21
15.8, 30.17, 4.546

Page 20
10.96, 17.45, 0.14
162.6, 6.477, 90.55
3378.28, 22.85, 3569.04
0.1, 0.713, 68.24
5755.82, 5.1, 18.69
52.73, 261.009, 411.7

Page 21
5.126, 3.08, 9.23
4255.5, 0.1, 8.749
633.599, 422.226, 42.79
7.259, 137.21, 18.37
0.903, 2112.4, 5.005
2.02, 38.3, 9493.3

Page 22
9.639, 86.9, 8.5
232.2, 5.31, 14.29
277.052, 186.82, 55.041
58.05, 1.577, 49.325
1.098, 7840.4, 9.654
67.006, 6.6, 13.739

Page 23
4345.6, 23.903, 7.659
708.35, 1.26, 2568.62
108.009, 9.88, 8.03
9.977, 10.445, 9.63
2.453, 0.54, 1411.8
0.71, 41.689, 56.27

Page 24
63.42, 3.635, 22.3
99.3, 1.518, 6490.81
41.1, 12.55, 868.5
37.058, 7.23, 365.02
9263.019, 0.012, 63.475
8.518, 92.9, 533.33

Page 25
847.2, 47.004, 70.34
7841.89, 89.2, 19.06
0.431, 6745.695, 0.152
1.45, 13.79, 99.47
14.09, 116.5, 416.2
616.023, 22.636, 5.682

Page 26
109.98, 7.955, 7.606
82.5, 7.16, 2.8
66.107, 2.492, 16.221
100, 6.43, 78.9
83.181, 115.9, 61.29
6584.2, 7.69, 5119.1

Part 2 Answers:

Page 28
0.596, 15.2, 7904.1
7.8, 7, 499.87
275.16, 0.012, 59.1
597.696, 0.87, 729.04
51.394, 1.41, 401.6
58.05, 2.115, 92.394

Page 29
5.802, 0.4, 0.837
3.442, 72.5, 75.992
0.666, 73.625, 3.37
0.413, 2.91, 27.8
7449.3, 2.498, 859.87
235.1, 40.149, 93.489

Page 30
2.7, 5.76, 157.2
1.994, 13.12, 42.287
91.55, 276.7, 259.995
4090.279, 0.033, 0.291
4.544, 2.3, 25.7
0.883, 66.89, 640.513

Page 31
93.998, 3.189, 5.41
6.086, 1.705, 5.399
0.688, 3930.8, 0.599
0.066, 0.01, 319.1
0.979, 25.991, 0.734
70.16, 177.218, 95.79

Page 32
0.693, 9.29, 66.17
2.981, 2.847, 7.58
72.5, 67.979, 5.024
0.03, 43.92, 96.234
57.992, 8811.5, 26.24
22.08, 321.496, 2.936

Page 33
3.514, 28.386, 631.64
88.8, 54.151, 5.8
6.896, 0.279, 983.665
3212.4, 87.95, 26.57
9.195, 3.669, 4178.8
36.44, 4.13, 62.56

Page 34
215.172, 0.14, 45.993
666.84, 2.467, 15.192
3.681, 3.015, 4.177
75.427, 4.93, 0.62
591.01, 0.38, 2.04
0.22, 1420.5, 4.185

Page 35
7517, 32.572, 3.999
43.204, 4.75, 740.4
724.902, 3744.3, 688.969
69.7, 2.06, 236.19
64.335, 1.4, 2.063
2.324, 56.837, 831.99

Page 36
3.55, 6865.33, 0.084
904.16, 845.1, 4.13
34.26, 697.269, 3.508
76.676, 10.6, 2.88
0.63, 31.026, 0.052
2.8, 7267.7, 4.2

Page 37
526.64, 0.694, 15.541
66.87, 8229.59, 3.963
4.619, 65.2, 8.071
7.805, 0.016, 157.798
1.704, 49.9, 79
7486.905, 918.5, 8.513

Page 38
98.047, 4.7, 1.5
67.49, 2.445, 2
321.25, 64.11, 902.1
4330.1, 16.55, 28.2
4, 0.394, 670.93
699.969, 0.12, 686.84

Page 39
3.995, 6.912, 15.79
329.79, 0.083, 459.9
4.815, 2734.7, 1746.993
60.7, 652.53, 9.21
9096.148, 352.586, 42.9
0.798, 374.29, 3.24

Page 40
15.974, 5.465, 6.252
4.54, 0.011, 445.033
404.4, 6.51, 48.994
13.982, 1.83, 0.081
56.81, 1545.8, 5.22
51.99, 868.1, 5.064

Page 41
70.42, 312.7, 7.99
0.003, 21.09, 59.3
727.859, 9.09, 28.25
2.175, 79.548, 54.999
2284.8, 6.93, 261.121
5.22, 26.92, 492.17

Page 42
7.74, 9.55, 0.025
87.04, 1.063, 460.83
9.38, 31.4, 523.6
1.476, 76.03, 0.37
14.45, 1.17, 11.996
11.5, 222.57, 1.07

Page 43
0.831, 567.5, 86.36
61.448, 36.19, 6.6
87.721, 5.46, 17.3
3.25, 0.13, 9.22
2.65, 270.1, 144.51
8566.25, 1137.951, 627.916

Page 44
854.6, 15.93, 0.068
219, 81.12, 0.14
0.357, 917, 43.44
4.293, 520.2, 536.6
8.413, 0.038, 122.73
3851.4, 1.529, 79.073

Page 45
0.039, 21.88, 7926.984
3.474, 79.935, 433.43
0.7, 0.99, 4.94
1686.166, 0.01, 0.943
0.313, 4.26, 8.7
429.092, 476.954, 5.4

Page 46
73.36, 0.581, 8.2
2675.892, 830.03, 6740.49
0.404, 5.995, 78.8
479.71, 0.144, 339.9
2.633, 794.95, 7.358
0.3, 34.52, 7199.8

Page 47
12.3, 4.69, 882.36
684.6, 42.988, 412
97.97, 71.906, 871.16
421.85, 120, 3.58
84.44, 618.363, 46.3
2.516, 1905.9, 0.12

Part 3 Answers:

Page 49
0.07735, 0.6464, 432
0.00006, 2.044, 2366
2.204, 0.00564, 4.296
226.746, 22.126, 71.744

Page 50
0.552, 214954.5, 399.28
504, 3172.16, 390.8
0.90428, 1.888, 0.043365
1.183, 8397.9, 69478.695

Page 51
17.25, 2.568, 28.662
331403.82, 0.03036, 19.44
2.641, 20430.256, 4.72
0.007, 0.8988, 0.58

Page 52
1.794, 5197.5, 53.0979
0.0014, 568, 11066.276
2094.6, 0.215, 1.876
0.106, 0.036, 46.472

Page 53
319.04, 3465.66, 3324.6
0.26341, 42.6624, 90.8658
66.42, 2.59, 888.72
154831, 2.1, 0.035

Page 54
2134.03, 245.63, 0.50676
293.46, 0.42, 1.432662
1024.003, 1.76, 2424.24
0.02877, 1.056, 1.11

Page 55
1.24, 1.12, 47864.08
3.172, 4513.925, 24616
0.0704, 229.8681, 0.033138
0.00585, 0.7128, 0.068

Page 56
460.8, 52.096, 0.0172
0.6, 0.0006, 0.06734
0.658, 2.45, 194.12
75.8, 88462.85, 4.5635

Page 57
69.04, 48.15, 7.99
116.28314, 1.07, 0.0546
0.346, 0.81, 0.387
72.096, 14.993, 2.226

Page 58
17.31, 24.09, 81346.418
7.632, 1.845, 1647.6
0.0095, 12359.12, 4.05
2270.8991, 14.324, 19761.918

Page 59
479.58, 2.36108, 13.26
1.796, 0.7322, 573.6939
31.164, 9.0219, 7.245
32.69, 6245.6, 30.6

Page 60
78800.2, 1737.16, 2712.45
4044.8, 9.618, 1820.39
0.114, 2550.4, 1019.35
67.0505, 576.2151, 0.21

Page 61
240, 7.79, 28316.952
0.922, 174.638, 2.0136
676.13, 460.5, 57.06
1.0619, 1.4134, 1.691

Page 62
5.5112, 0.0048, 11.2
12, 0.00096, 0.054
0.005, 2001, 0.12
0.000552, 0.037368, 5.328

Page 63
36868.28, 50866.2, 1871.22
59.0446, 4115, 7659.232
0.07762, 8.168, 114.9
9.212, 361.92, 1.383

Page 64
0.056, 65.262, 1.151
0.4, 3.542287, 0.00012
187.488, 32.28918, 3859795.8
23511.6, 0.0034, 0.97888

Page 65
124.44, 37.8, 1.923
471.861, 0.000006, 0.000174
11223.6, 577090.14, 0.24
47.61, 5.232, 27.006

Page 66
0.1944, 2.8, 42
17.4363, 10095.53, 0.000315
3.675, 0.0192, 698.16
72.9, 0.054, 8.39792

Page 67
369.6, 9.72, 0.144
0.19397, 0.98, 10.382
733.8, 2984.5, 0.0069
526.252, 2590.2, 0.0014

Page 68
1.9782, 2719528.8, 0.02
0.64, 23859, 358.5208
18.9224, 3620.5, 44080.4
2690.28, 13.66, 1.075

Part 4 Answers:

Page 70
8.4, 37, 71
8.77, 0.07, 0.9
0.06, 7.6, 0.75
76.6, 0.3, 0.93

Page 71
7, 0.24, 6
8.65, 3.3, 0.6
25.1, 0.6, 3.4
9, 0.2, 0.01

Page 72
458, 0.04, 41
1.29, 0.4, 7
21, 9, 1.75
6, 61.2, 0.3

Page 73
1.9, 0.03, 0.2
0.05, 44, 0.7
1.72, 0.46, 88.8
6, 0.08, 0.05

Page 74
1.1, 0.06, 857
0.58, 87.2, 0.02
0.3, 7.2, 82.1
8.62, 0.01, 73

Page 75
0.31, 0.03, 5.2
0.05, 0.3, 1
84.8, 8, 684
9.98, 9.4, 19.3

Page 76
3.9, 2.3, 2.4
3.1, 0.05, 75.6
0.4, 0.04, 67
8.65, 0.03, 0.01

Practice Arithmetic with Decimals Workbook

Page 77
0.04, 2.72, 4
9.5, 3.9, 0.8
246, 1.7, 3.7
85.7, 0.1, 0.93

Page 78
5, 74, 1.09
0.06, 29, 0.5
4.5, 2.4, 7.8
602, 0.4, 9

Page 79
98, 2, 97
0.04, 4.1, 9.7
0.06, 85.9, 0.29
9.04, 0.05, 8.9

Page 80
0.06, 0.4, 0.06
4.3, 3.11, 430
0.06, 40, 0.07
3.4, 37, 86.8

Page 81
0.39, 0.4, 2.6
0.8, 0.04, 8.1
0.19, 7.6, 9.22
1, 988, 0.04

Page 82
51, 0.59, 2.9
0.02, 9.8, 0.53
8.7, 3.6, 990
0.07, 0.1, 0.34

Page 83
0.1, 4.9, 8
2, 61.9, 0.31
3, 0.23, 0.8
0.4, 20, 0.15

Page 84
27.7, 84.8, 0.99
8.6, 0.07, 0.1
7, 29, 0.74
0.4, 0.8, 58

Page 85
459, 3, 0.7
0.96, 2.6, 0.5
8.5, 0.13, 0.08
0.69, 6.62, 70.2

Page 86
0.74, 0.6, 0.4
83.8, 0.4, 7
35.2, 8.8, 0.04
9.33, 7.99, 0.5

Page 87
3, 0.34, 0.04
6.35, 28.9, 0.05
21, 0.2, 9.6
0.33, 0.7, 0.99

Page 88
0.06, 0.69, 0.04
0.57, 0.03, 4.83
82, 7, 4.28
0.1, 3.8, 0.9

Page 89
0.64, 805, 7.2
0.03, 839, 0.9
8, 46.8, 5.6
7.5, 0.04, 7.8

117

Part 5 Answers:

Note: A bar above a number or sequence of numbers indicates repeating decimals. For example, $0.\overline{3} = 0.333333333...$ The digit 3 in this decimal repeats forever. As another example, $0.00\overline{36} = 0.003636363636...$. This time, the sequence 36 repeats forever.

If the decimal sequence has not started to repeat by the 9th decimal position, the number has been rounded to the nearest billionth. Although such precision is given here, it would be reasonable for the student to carry the answers out only to a handful of significant figures.

Page 91
0.306122449, 0.638297872, 0.625
9.8, 3.$\overline{8}$, 76
0.019534884, 0.8$\overline{27}$, 0.553424658
0.07, 22.14285714, 0.880952381

Page 92
4.3, 5, 0.97
0.0004$\overline{16}$, 0.053061224, 2.9$\overline{6}$
5.$\overline{714285}$, 5.5, 3.0875
0.$\overline{219780}$, 362.5, 0.158$\overline{3}$

Page 93
9.9$\overline{714285}$, 0.$\overline{7692307}$, 0.07813186
0.174509804, 0.30$\overline{3}$, 0.02$\overline{272}$
19.4$\overline{3}$, 2.39$\overline{4}$, 4.05
54.92957746, 0.0525, 0.2

Page 94
2.35$\overline{12195}$, 0.2, 0.0$\overline{461538}$
0.155172414, 0.$\overline{1230769}$, 0.01125
0.56, 3.2, 90.8$\overline{57142}$
78.8, 2.608695652, 3.5

Page 95
31, 23.975, 14.4
0.$\overline{36}$, 1.0$\overline{2}$, 1.842105263
8, 0.04, 0.0$\overline{2}$
4, 0.001694915, 0.539473684

Page 96
1.18, 0.5, 1.070588235
0.005$\overline{16483}$, 0.25, 2.25
0.0006$\overline{0}$, 0.106451613, 3.673469388
0.15, 5.011764706, 0.104

Page 97
0.00$\overline{12195}$, 3.1$\overline{6}$, 0.084337349
38, 0.007865169, 0.000140845
111.$\overline{428571}$, 0.117647059, 240
0.23125, 1.2, 0.001836735

Page 98
0.0208$\overline{3}$, 0.0862$\overline{5}$, 7.2
0.045789474, 0.034482759, 0.0$\overline{01}$
9.5, 10.$\overline{4}$, 2.0$\overline{6}$
133.$\overline{3}$, 0.131578947, 701.$\overline{1}$

Page 99
0.047058824, 0.518072289, 62.4$\overline{32}$
0.5$\overline{571428}$, 0.021428571, 0.1$\overline{3}$
0.5$\overline{3}$, 0.$\overline{5}$, 1.88
1.1$\overline{371428}$5, 0.335, 0.01875

Page 100
7, 3.75, 0.00384615
0.013$\overline{8}$, 1.25, 0.031$\overline{36}$
16.4, 0.195652174, 0.013728814
0.003728814, 0.05, 10.068$\overline{1}$

Page 101
17.34693878, 0.893617021, 0.002
6.$\overline{6}$, 1.37, 0.056701031
0.076086957, 1.$\overline{371428}$5, 105.$\overline{5}$
35.40983607, 0.8, 0.055434783

Page 102
0.00$\overline{238095}$, 9.32, 0.08$\overline{3}$
0.010526316, 70.$\overline{1}$, 0.02$\overline{8}$
0.$\overline{5}$, 19.5, 11.125
6.7, 0.45, 48.6

Page 103
1040, 8, 2.19230769
1, 9.3, 0.041$\overline{6}$
0.02, 39.$\overline{428571}$, 5.$\overline{74}$
0.008928571, 0.01, 0.201578947

Page 104
2.647058824, 193.$\overline{3}$, 5790
6, 0.52, 11.1$\overline{857142}$
1.$\overline{0809523}$, 1, 7.86$\overline{3}$
0.$\overline{571428}$, 0.068, 0.0$\overline{428571}$

Page 105
11.$\overline{6}$, 0.079569892, 190
0.708928571, 19.64, 0.028125
14.2, 0.000309278, 0.04$\overline{36585}$
4.25, 1, 0.53$\overline{8}$

Page 106
13.$\overline{3}$, 0.0$\overline{4}$, 0.625
1.$\overline{2142857}$, 0.103448276, 1.11
9.52, 0.016206897, 1.$\overline{168831}$
0.2, 0.00$\overline{743902}$, 0.035068493

Page 107
1.011235955, 11.9$\overline{428571}$, 0.77
0.04, 0.00$\overline{809523}$, 0.0197$\overline{916}$
0.06, 1.640625, 1.11
0.005, 0.1, 0.695180723

Page 108
2.54, 0.339$\overline{285714}$, 1.$\overline{6}$
0.1, 0.$\overline{5}$, 0.124637681
0.824137931, 290, 1727.5
10.$\overline{1}$, 76.1$\overline{3}$, 0.001

Page 109
4.573684211, 0.15, 4.2875

4, 0.1, 0.$\overline{705479452}$

1.23$\overline{8}$, 0.17$\overline{5}$, 0.8$\overline{5}$

69.8$\overline{3}$, 0.32$\overline{5}$, 0.10$\overline{3}$

Page 110
8.2$\overline{3}$, 4.$\overline{90}$, 0.1$\overline{6857142}$

11.125, 35.84210526, 0.015217391

0.003448276, 0.052631579, 0.1$\overline{3}$

0.060493827, 0.2$\overline{285714}$, 0.3$\overline{8}$

Printed in Great Britain
by Amazon